'I am not sure that, as a maverick Christian, I am in the least competent to comment on Dr Williams's book *Being Christian*, but I have read it with great interest and admiration. It is indeed a privilege to enter into the mind of one of the most distinguished theologians of the modern age, a former Archbishop of Canterbury whose life and work have been rooted in his Christian belief. The book deals in what have been seen, since the formation of the Church, as the essentials of Christianity – baptism, Bible, Eucharist and prayer – which, despite the variety, particularly today in Christian thinking and practice, convinced Christians see as indispensible elements of their faith. Dr Williams also addresses some of the questions that, for generations, have occupied and sometimes perplexed the minds of believers. He is discussing matters that are necessarily complex, but the style is elegant and lucid, and the book, although written primarily for Christians, will be interesting and helpful to those who are seekers after, rather than finders of, religious faith.'

P. D. James, OBE, FRSA, FRSL, novelist

'Unless we understand our faith we cannot live it, but it is the living that matters. Knowing and thinking and understanding are all means to draw us into the life of Christ, an active living and loving way of being. Christianity is both simple and profound. Rowan Williams understands these two levels and how we come to the depth of what Jesus is by the simplicities of informed Christian practice. This is a handbook for Christian living.'

Sister Wendy Beckett, Carmelite Monastery, Quidenham, Norfolk

'Who better than Rowan Williams to be our teacher about the essentials of Christianity! In this clear, accessible exposition, we get Williams at his best . . . worldly-wise, pastorally gentle, grounded deeply in tradition, acutely alert to the real world of violence where God indwells. Williams ushers us more deeply into our best discernment of the Christian life.'

Walter Brueggemann, Emeritus Professor of Old Testament,
Columbia Theological Seminary

'Full of rich metaphor and the sort of insight you want to spend a week reflecting on, Rowan Williams's *Being Christian* offers a succinct introduction to four core elements of Christian life. The book offers a vision of the Christian life that is both challenging and attractive as we are encouraged to be "in the heart of a needy, contaminated, messy world" as well as encouraging an authenticity of life. Very readable yet profound, *Being Christian* has potential to be formational for those preparing for confirmation or waiting to understand what it means to be a Christian.'

Sally Nash, Director of Midlands Centre for Youth Ministry, St John's College, Nottingham

'Young people need to hear about the essentials of Christian faith from someone who knows them inside out. In this thought-provoking book, Rowan Williams shares the riches of his wonderful mind in a way that will inform, stretch and inspire people of all ages and backgrounds. But young people, especially, will find this book invaluable as they take their next step of faith.'

Jenny Baker, Development Manager, Church Urban Fund

'With remarkable clarity, depth and simplicity, Rowan Williams takes us into the heart of what it means to be Christian. A lifetime's immersion in the classics of Christian theology and devotion lies hidden behind this fresh and illuminating sketch of the essentials, its shape guided by tradition and its lines drawn from personal experience of Christian living and praying.'

Frances Young, Emeritus Professor of Theology, University of Birmingham

'This is what you get when someone who is both very learned and a former Archbishop of Canterbury writes about what Christians share in practice, but does so from the perspective of living as an ordinary, flawed Christian disciple himself. Simple and engaging enough to read at a sitting, *Being Christian* is also profound and provocative enough to provide material for fruitful reflection – and action – for the whole of our Christian life.

No doubt this book will frequently be given as a most acceptable confirmation present, but I think it should also be read by those of us who have been around the block a bit with the Church, and probably thought we had already grasped the whole point of the exercise.'

Janet Morley, author, speaker and worship leader

Born in 1950, Rowan Williams was educated in Swansea (Wales) and Cambridge. He studied for his theology doctorate in Oxford, after which he taught theology in a seminary near Leeds. From 1977 until 1986, he was engaged in academic and parish work in Cambridge, before returning to Oxford as Lady Margaret Professor of Divinity. In 1990 he became a fellow of the British Academy.

In 1992 Professor Williams became Bishop of Monmouth, and in 1999 he was elected as Archbishop of Wales. He became Archbishop of Canterbury in late 2002 with ten years' experience as a diocesan bishop and three as a primate in the Anglican Communion. As archbishop, his main responsibilities were pastoral – whether leading his own diocese of Canterbury and the Church of England, or guiding the Anglican Communion worldwide. At the end of 2012, after ten years as archbishop, he stepped down and moved to a new role as Master of Magdalene College, Cambridge.

Professor Williams is acknowledged internationally as an outstanding theological writer and teacher as well as an accomplished poet and translator. His interests include music, fiction and languages.

BEING CHRISTIAN

Baptism, Bible, Eucharist, Prayer

Rowan Williams

First published in Great Britain in 2014

Society for Promoting Christian Knowledge
36 Causton Street
London SW1P 4ST
www.spckpublishing.co.uk

British Library Cataloguing-in-Publication Data
A catalogue record for this book is available from the British Library

ISBN 978-0-281-07171-5
eBook ISBN 978-0-281-07173-9

Typeset by Data Standards Ltd, Frome, Somerset

First printed in Great Britain by Ashford Colour Press
Subsequently digitally printed in Great Britain

eBook by Data Standards Ltd, Frome, Somerset

Produced on paper from sustainable forests

Contents

Introduction ix

1 Baptism 1

2 Bible 21

3 Eucharist 41

4 Prayer 61

Suggestions for further reading 83

Introduction

What are the essential elements of the Christian life? I am not thinking in terms of individuals leading wonderful lives, but just in terms of those simple and recognizable things that make you realize that you are part of a Christian community. This little book is designed to help you think about four of the most obvious of these things: baptism, Bible, Eucharist and prayer.

Christians are received into full membership of the Church by having water poured or sprinkled over them (or, in some traditions, being fully immersed); Christians read the Bible; Christians gather to share bread and wine in memory of the death and resurrection of Jesus of Nazareth; and Christians pray. There is a huge and bewildering variety in Christian thinking and practice about all kinds of things, but these four basic activities have remained constant and indispensable for the majority of those who call themselves Christians.

In this book we shall be looking at what those activities tell us about the essence of Christian life, and what kind of people we might hope to become in a community where these things are done.

These chapters are based on talks given in Canterbury Cathedral as part of a regular series of open lectures during Holy Week. I am very grateful to Jonathan and Sarah Goodall for all their work in transcribing and editing these talks and for further generous help from Philip Law at SPCK in preparing them for publication.

Rowan Williams
Cambridge, Advent 2013

1

Baptism

> Do you not know that all of us who have been baptized into Christ Jesus were baptized into his death? Therefore we have been buried with him by baptism into death, so that, just as Christ was raised from the dead by the glory of the Father, so we too might walk in newness of life. (Romans 6.3–4)

We begin with baptism: with the fact that people are formally brought into the Christian community by being dipped in water or having water poured over them.

The word 'baptism' originally just meant 'dipping'. If we turn to the New Testament we find this word featuring in the ministry and teaching of Jesus, and also, quite extensively, in St Paul's letters. Jesus speaks of the suffering and death that lies ahead of him as a 'baptism' he is going to endure (Mark 10.38). That is, he speaks as if his going towards suffering and death were a kind of immersion in something, being drowned or swamped in something. He has, he says, an 'immersion' to go through, and until it is completed he will be frustrated and his work will be incomplete (Luke 12.50). So it seems that, from the very beginning, baptism as a ritual for joining the Christian community was associated with the idea of going down into the darkness of Jesus' suffering and death, being 'swamped' by the reality of what Jesus endured. St Paul speaks of being baptized 'into' the death of Christ (Romans 6.3). We are, so to speak, 'dropped' into that mysterious event which Christians commemorate on Good Friday, and, more regularly, in the breaking of bread at Holy Communion.

Out of the depths

As the Church began to reflect a bit more on this in the early Christian centuries, as it began to shape its liturgy and its art, another set of associations developed. In the story of Jesus' baptism he goes down into the water of the River Jordan, and as he comes up out of the water the Holy Spirit descends upon him in the form of a dove and a voice speaks from heaven: 'You are my Son' (Luke 3.22). Reflecting on that story, the early Christians soon began to make connections with another story involving water and the Spirit. At the very beginning of creation, the book of Genesis tells us, there was watery chaos. And over that watery chaos there was, depending on how you read the Hebrew, the Holy Spirit hovering or a great wind blowing (or perhaps one is a sort of metaphor for the other). First there is chaos, and then there is the wind of

God's Spirit; and out of the watery chaos comes the world. And God says, 'This is good.' The water and the Spirit and the voice: you can see why the early Christians began to associate the event of baptism with exactly that image which St Paul uses for the Christian life – new creation.

So the beginning of Christian life is a new beginning of God's creative work. And just as Jesus came up out of the water, receiving the Spirit and hearing the voice of the Father, so for the newly baptized Christian the voice of God says, 'You are my son/daughter', as that individual begins his or her new life in association with Jesus.

In the tradition of the Christian East especially, when the baptism of Jesus is shown in icons you will usually see Jesus up to his neck in the water, while below, sitting under the waves, are the river gods of the old world, representing the chaos that is being overcome. So from very early on baptism is drawing around itself a set of very powerful symbols. Water and rebirth: rebirth as a son or daughter of God, as Jesus himself is a son; chaos moving into order as the wind of God blows upon it.

So it is not surprising that as the Church reflected on what baptism means, it came to view it as a kind of restoration of what it is to be truly human. To be baptized is to recover the humanity that God first intended. What did God intend? He intended that human beings should

To be baptized is to recover the humanity that God first intended

grow into such love for him and such confidence in him that they could rightly be called God's sons and daughters. Human beings have let go of that identity, abandoned it, forgotten it or corrupted it. And when Jesus arrives on the scene he restores humanity to where it should be. But that in itself means that Jesus, as he restores humanity 'from within' (so to speak), has to come down into the chaos of our human world. Jesus has to come down fully to our level, to where things are shapeless and meaningless, in a state of vulnerability and unprotectedness, if real humanity is to come to birth.

This suggests that the new humanity that is created around Jesus is not a humanity that is always going to be successful and in control of things, but a humanity that can reach out its hand from the depths of chaos, to be touched by the hand of God. And that means that if we ask the question, 'Where might you expect to find the baptized?' one answer is, 'In the neighbourhood of chaos'. It means you might expect to find Christian people near to those places where humanity is most at risk, where humanity is most disordered, disfigured and needy. Christians will be found in the neighbourhood of Jesus – but Jesus is found in the neighbourhood of human confusion and suffering, defencelessly alongside those in need. If being baptized is being led to where Jesus is, then being baptized is being led towards the chaos and the neediness of a humanity that has forgotten its own destiny.

I am inclined to add that you might also expect the baptized Christian to be somewhere near, somewhere in touch with, the chaos in his or her own life – because we all of us live not just with a chaos outside ourselves but with quite a lot of inhumanity and muddle inside us. A baptized Christian ought to be somebody who is not afraid of looking with honesty at that chaos inside, as well as being where humanity is at risk, outside.

So baptism means being with Jesus 'in the depths': the depths of human need, including the depths of our own selves in their need – but also in the depths of God's love; in the depths where the Spirit is re-creating and refreshing human life as God meant it to be.

Sharing in the life and death of Jesus

If all this is correct, baptism does not confer on us a status that marks us off from everybody else. To be able to say, 'I'm baptized' is not to claim an extra dignity, let alone a sort of privilege that keeps you separate from and

Baptism does not confer on us a status that marks us off from everybody else

superior to the rest of the human race, but to claim a new level of solidarity with other people. It is to accept that to be a Christian is to be affected – you might even say *contaminated* – by the mess of humanity. This is very paradoxical. Baptism is a ceremony in which we are washed, cleansed and re-created. It is also a ceremony in which we are pushed into the middle of a human situation that may hurt us, and that will not leave us untouched or unsullied. And the gathering of baptized people is therefore not a convocation of those who are privileged, elite and separate, but of those who have accepted what it means to be in the heart of a needy, contaminated, messy world. To put it another way, you don't go down into the waters of the Jordan without stirring up a great deal of mud!

When we are brought to be where Jesus is in baptism we let our defences down so as to be where he is, in the depths of human chaos. And that means letting our defences down before God. Openness to the Spirit comes as we go with Jesus to take this risk of love and solidarity. And that is why, as we come up out of the waters of baptism with Jesus, we hear what he hears: 'This is my son, this is my daughter, this is the one who has the right to call me Father.' The Spirit, says St Paul, is always giving us the power to call God Father, and to pray Jesus' prayer (Galatians 4.6). And the baptized are these who, going with Jesus into risk and darkness, open themselves up to receive the Spirit that allows them to call God Father.

So what else do you expect to see in the baptized? An openness to human need, but also a corresponding openness to the Holy Spirit. In the life of baptized people, there is a constant rediscovering, re-enacting of the Father's embrace of Jesus in the Holy Spirit. The baptized person is not only in the middle of human suffering and muddle but in the middle of the love and delight of the Father, the Son and the Holy Spirit. That surely is one of the most extraordinary mysteries of being Christian. We are in the middle of two things that seem quite contradictory: in the middle of the heart of God, the ecstatic joy of the Father, the Son and the Holy Spirit; and in the middle of a world of threat, suffering, sin and pain. And because Jesus has taken his stand right in the middle of those two realities, that is where we take ours. As he says, 'Where I am, there will my servant be also' (John 12.26).

Growing out of that, the prayer of baptized people is going to be a prayer that is always moving in the depths, sometimes invisibly – a prayer that comes from places deeper than we can really understand. St Paul says just this in his letter to the Romans: 'The Spirit helps us in our weakness ... that very Spirit intercedes with sighs too deep for words' (Romans 8.26). The prayer of baptized people is never just 'rattling off' the words at surface level. The prayer of baptized people comes from a place deeper than we can penetrate with our minds or even our feelings. Prayer in the baptized community surges up from the depths of God's own life. Or, to change the metaphor, you might say that we are carried along on a tide deeper than ourselves, welling up from God's depths and the world's.

The prayer of baptized people is a growing and moving into the prayer of Jesus himself and therefore it is a prayer that may often be difficult and mysterious. It will not always be cheerful and clear, and it may not always feel as though it is going to be answered. Christians do not pray expecting to get what they ask for in any simple sense – you just might have noticed that this can't be taken for granted! Rather, Christians pray because they *have* to, because the Spirit is surging up inside them. Prayer, in other words, is more like sneezing – there comes a point where you can't not do it. The Spirit wells and surges up towards God the Father. But because of this there will be moments when, precisely because you can't help yourself, it can feel dark and unrewarding, deeply puzzling, hard to speak about.

Which is why so many great Christian writers on the spiritual life have emphasized that prayer is not about feeling good. It is not about results, or about being pleased with yourself; it is just what God does *in* you when you are close to Jesus. And that of course means that the path of the baptized person is a dangerous one. Perhaps baptism really ought to have some health warnings attached to it: 'If you take this step, if you go into these depths, it will be transfiguring, exhilarating, life-giving and very, very dangerous.' To be baptized into Jesus is not to be in what the world thinks of as a safe place. Jesus' first disciples discovered that in the Gospels, and his disciples have gone on discovering it ever since.

One of the great privileges of my time as Archbishop of Canterbury was being allowed to go and see some of those places at close quarters where people live in dangerous proximity to Jesus; where their witness means they are at risk in various ways. And when you see people in places like Zimbabwe, Sudan, Syria or Pakistan living both in the neighbourhood of Jesus and in the neighbourhood of great danger, you understand something of what commitment to the Christian life means, the commitment of which baptism is the sign. But you see it also when you look at the lives of great saints whose path of contemplation has led them to deep inner desolation, loneliness and uncertainty (think of what Mother Teresa of Calcutta wrote in her diaries about the many years in which she felt practically no 'spiritual' comfort, only isolation and darkness). All this results from the upsurging life of the Spirit in the centre of our being, coming from the heart of God. Like the saints before us, we tread a dangerous path – which is also the path to life.

Like the saints before us, we tread a dangerous path – which is also the path to life

The path is both dangerous and life-giving for me as an individual believer – but not only for me. The other great truth about baptism is that it brings you into proximity not only with God the Father, not only with the suffering and muddle of the human world, but with all those other people who are invited to be there as well. Baptism brings you into the neighbourhood of other Christians; and there is no way of being a Christian without being in the neighbourhood of other Christians. Bad news for many, because other Christians can be so difficult! But that is what the New Testament tells us very uncompromisingly: to be with Jesus is to be where human suffering and pain are found, and it is also to be with other human beings who are invited to be with Jesus. And that, says the New Testament, is a gift as well as sometimes a struggle and an embarrassment.

It is a gift because in this community of baptized people we receive life from others' prayer and love, and we give the prayer and love that others need. We are caught up in a great economy of giving and exchange.

The solidarity that baptism brings us into, the solidarity with suffering, is a solidarity with one another as well. It is what some Christian writers have called, in a rather forbidding word, 'co-inherence'. We are 'implicated' in one another, our lives are interwoven. What affects one Christian affects all, what affects all affects each one. And, whether as individual Christians or as individual Christian groups and denominations, we often find that hard to believe and accept. We find it hard to accept it as a gift – yet a gift is what it is. It means that the darkness that belongs in the baptized life is never my own problem exclusively. It is shared: how it is shared is very mysterious, and yet most of us who are baptized Christians can witness in one way or another to the fact that it works.

We are 'implicated' in one another, our lives are interwoven

So baptism restores a human identity that has been forgotten or overlaid. Baptism takes us to where Jesus is. It takes us therefore into closer neighbourhood with a dark and fallen world, and it takes us into closer neighbourhood with others invited there. The baptized life is characterized by solidarity with those in need, and sharing with all others who believe. And it is characterized by a prayerfulness that courageously keeps going, even when things are difficult and unpromising and unrewarding, simply because you cannot stop the urge to pray. Something keeps coming alive in you; never mind the results.

Prophets, priests and kings

I want to explore just a little further what this baptized identity, this new humanity, means by considering three of the titles that are often used in thinking about the identity of Jesus. For many centuries the Church has thought of Jesus as anointed by God to live out a threefold identity: that of prophet, priest and king. The baptized person identifies with Jesus in these three ways of being human which characterize and define his unique humanity. As we grow into his life and humanity these three ways come to characterize us as well. The life of the baptized is a life of prophecy and priesthood and royalty. What does this mean for those of us who do not normally think of our roles in quite such dramatic terms?

First, think about the role of the prophet. What do prophets do in the Old Testament? They of course do more than just foretell the future. Much more importantly, they act and speak to call the people of Israel back to their own essential truth and identity. They act and they speak for the sake of a community's integrity, its faithfulness to who it is really meant to be. Isaiah and Jeremiah and Amos and Hosea are constantly saying to the people of Israel, 'Don't you remember who you are? Don't you remember what God has called you to be? Here you are, sitting down comfortably with all kinds of inequality, injustice and corruption in your society. Have you completely forgotten what you're here for?'

The prophet, therefore, is somebody whose role is always to be challenging the community to be what it is meant to be – to live out the gift that God has given to it. And so the baptized person, reflecting the prophetic role of Jesus Christ, is a person who needs to be critical, who needs to be a questioner. The baptized person looks around at the Church and may quite often be prompted to say, 'Have you forgotten what you're here for?'; 'Have you forgotten the gift God gave you?'

And one of the very uncomfortable roles we have to play in the Church is to be prophets to one another – that is, to remind *one another* what we are here for. By that I don't mean that every Christian needs to go around nagging every other Christian (attractive as that might be to some kinds of people). I mean rather that we need to be, in a variety of ways, ready to show one another what the integrity of Christian life is about. It is much more a case of nudging one another from time to time and saying, 'What do you see?'; 'What's your vision?'; 'What are you making yourself accountable to?' And to go on gently holding one another accountable before God doesn't mean nagging or censoriousness. It means something much more like a quiet, persistent re-calling of one another to what is most important. We do it silently every time we meet for worship. We do it, ideally, when we meet together privately. We do it in all sorts of ways. The Church needs always to hear that critical voice saying, 'Back to the beginning, back to where it all comes from. Let's try and listen again to what God first said to us.' So, as prophets we lead one another back to the essentials: back to baptism, Bible, Holy Communion and prayer.

But if we as prophets are gifted with this uncomfortable calling to ask questions of one another, what about the wider societies we live in? People speak rather loosely of the Church being 'prophetic' and sometimes people talk as if the prophetic role of the Church is simply a matter of taking loud and very clear stands on all the issues of the day. But it is surely much more a matter of the Church expressing and asking important and readily forgotten questions in our society. It is to ask, 'What's that for?' and 'Why do we take that for granted?' and 'Where's that leading us?' We do it for one another in the Church but I think that we also do it for the whole of our human environment, which needs that sort of questioning for its health and survival.

What about the priestly role? Again, we go back to the Bible. In the Old Testament a priest is somebody who interprets God and humanity to each other. A priest is somebody who builds bridges between God and humanity when that relationship has been wrecked; somebody who by offering sacrifice to God re-creates a shattered relationship. Of Jesus' priestly role I need hardly speak in that connection. But you will perhaps see how, as baptized people are drawn into the priestliness of Jesus, they are called upon to mend shattered relationships between God and the world, through the power of Christ and his Spirit. As baptized people, we are in the business of building bridges. We are in the business, once again, of seeing situations where there is breakage, damage and disorder, and bringing into those situations the power of God in Jesus Christ and the Holy Spirit in order to rebuild something. We may not offer sacrifices in the Old Testament sense but we offer and bring before God the reality of Jesus which has restored everything. We pray in Jesus that that restoration may apply here, and here, and here. And we offer our own service and devotion as best we can in the bridge-building process.

As baptized people, we are in the business of building bridges

And the gift of 'royalty'? In ancient Israel, the king was somebody who spoke for others to God. The king himself had a priestly role. But the king had the freedom to shape the law and the justice of his society. He could keep people close to the demands of God's covenant; he could make justice a reality (or, of course, fail terribly in this task). We read in Jeremiah the great definition of what it means to be a king who will 'know God' by favouring the poor, doing justice for the needy (Jeremiah 22.16). And that 'royal' calling is about how we freely engage in shaping our lives and our human environment in the direction of God's justice, showing in our relationships and our engagement with the world something of God's own freedom, God's own liberty to heal and restore.

So the baptized life is a life that gives us the resource and strength to ask awkward but necessary questions of one another and of our world. It is a life that looks towards reconciliation, building bridges, repairing shattered relationships. It is a life that looks towards justice and liberty, the liberty to work together to make human life in society some kind of reflection of the wisdom and order and justice of God.

All these aspects of the baptized life need one another. If we were *only* called to be prophets, we would be in danger of being constantly shrill nay-sayers to one another and to the world. There is plenty of that in Christian history, and plenty of that in the Christian mentality today. And if we were *only* priestly, there would be a danger of never asking the difficult questions but moving on as rapidly as we could to reconciliation; let's forget the difficult middle bit, let's get to the end of the story. And if we were *only* talking about royal freedom and justice we would be in danger of constantly thinking in terms of control and problem-solving. But just as in Jesus these three things are inseparably bound up in his work and his words and his death, as in his life, so for us these are three facets of one life, not three isolated bits of a vocation.

... but still sinners

Throughout Christian history there have been plenty of debates around baptism. In the early Church people debated whether it was possible to sin after baptism. The great temptation was to think that when you had entered the new creation, the old world just stopped existing. St Paul knew that temptation, but he also knew very well that the old world is tough, a natural survivor, and that the old humanity – muddled about its destiny and forgetful about its true nature – goes on with remarkable persistence.

So if, as a baptized person, you still sin – don't panic! Remember that the depths of God's love still surround you. And when you sin as a baptized person you are not, as it were, stepping right outside the depths of God's love (unless, of course, you fully and consciously decide to do so). Rather, it is as though you are deliberately ignoring the depths all around you, and not letting the reality of the world's need and the reality of God's love come through. So, what you need to do is to take the shutters down again, and you will find that every prayer of penitence that you pray is a taking-down of the shutters and letting the baptismal depths well up around and within you again.

And that brings us right back to where we started: the chaos of human sin and disorder and the wind of the Spirit blowing over it, and the embodied love of God going down into the waters and being drawn out again in a blaze of light and a word from heaven, 'This is my Son!' The baptized community lives in that mystery, drawn out of chaos, breathing in the wind of the Spirit and hearing from God the words that he speaks to his only Son: 'You can call me Father.'

For reflection or discussion

1 In what ways did Jesus immerse himself in the depths of God and humanity, and in what ways might you follow his example?
2 How might you or your church act as a mediator or bridge-builder between particular people or groups in your neighbourhood?

3 Have you sometimes felt a barrier or shutter go up between you and God? If so, what would you say has helped, or might help, to remove that barrier and allow God back in again?

2

Bible

> All scripture is inspired by God and is useful for teaching, for reproof, for correction, and for training in righteousness, so that everyone who belongs to God may be proficient, equipped for every good work. (2 Timothy 3.16–17)

In this chapter we are going to turn to an activity by which baptized people are very often most readily recognizable. One of the things that Christian people characteristically do is read the Bible – or rather, in quite a lot of circumstances, they have the Bible read to them. It is worth remembering, especially for us who are inheritors of the Reformation and part of a literate culture, that for the huge majority of Christians throughout the centuries, as well as for many today, the Bible is a book *heard* more than read. And that is quite a significant fact about it. For when you see a group of baptized people listening to the Bible in public worship, you realize that Bible-reading is an essential part of the Christian life because *Christian life is a listening life*. Christians are people who expect to be spoken to by God. And that is

Christians are people who expect to be spoken to by God

the underlying theme that I want to explore in this chapter.

The baptized Christian is someone who is in the habit not just of speaking to God, but of listening – indeed, listening *so as* to be able to speak. The Christian listens for God and listens in the company of other believers to those texts that, from the very beginnings of the Christian community, have been identified as carrying the voice of God. Our visual model of Bible-reading is probably still very much formed by the idea of a person sitting alone in a room with a bound volume. But that is a very modern and minority approach to the Bible. In the early Christian centuries it is almost certainly the case that most churches could never have afforded a complete text of the Bible.

If you think of the vast expense of copying out manuscripts in the ancient world, and of the number of manuscripts you have to copy out to get a complete Bible, you will understand why the ancient world was not awash, as we are, with spare Bibles. People *learned* the Bible. They recited it to one another. They copied out stretches of it, often from memory. That is why there are so many slightly faulty quotations from the Bible in early Christian literature, because not even then were people's memories perfect. They assembled collections of Sunday readings.

But complete Bibles? Probably only in the biggest churches and certainly not in the pocket of the individual Christian. Putting several dozen scrolls into your pocket would never have been very easy, in any case.

Now I say this not to deny the importance of all Christians having a Bible in their pocket with which they are familiar, but to point out that very often we make a set of assumptions about what is central and most important for Bible reading, which would have been quite strange in many parts of the Christian world for many centuries. And it still is strange to many of our fellow Christians today. It is very moving indeed when you see how Bibles are valued in poorer churches where you cannot just go and buy them in a bookshop. Some years ago the diocese where I then worked in Wales made a Lenten project of providing a Bible *from* every parish in the diocese *for* every parish in the Diocese of Lango in northern Uganda. And the response was very moving and warm, as you can imagine.

Hearing God's voice

The Bible is the territory in which Christians expect to hear God speaking. That is what the Church says about the Bible, and the Bible itself declares that it communicates what God wants to tell us. But that has always been a slightly complicated claim. Pick up a Bible; open it at random, and it is not very likely that the first thing you hit upon is a statement from God to you in a simple grammatical sense. You may hit upon a psalm: that is, a text of human address to God. You may hit upon a piece of history. You may indeed hit on one of those famously long and difficult family trees that crop up in the Bible, and you might wonder exactly what God might be saying to you in the statement that 'Unto Enoch was born Irad: and Irad begat Mehujael: and Mehujael begat Methusael . . .' (Genesis 4.18, KJV). You may hit upon an arresting, piercing, converting word of Jesus to his disciples. You may hit upon a complicated argument in a letter of St Paul. But you soon discover that what the Bible is *not* is a single sequence of instructions, beginning 'God says to you . . .'

There is not very much, in the plain grammatical sense, that is addressed directly to an audience. So what is going on? Here is a collection of books that includes, among other things, codes of law, collections of proverbial wisdom, hymnbooks, poetry (including love poetry), chronicles, letters, polemical texts attacking society, and visionary records. The diversity of the Bible is as great as if you had within the same two covers, for example, Shakespeare's sonnets, the law reports of 1910, the introduction to Kant's *Critique of Pure Reason*, the letters of St Anselm and a fragment of *The Canterbury Tales. All within the same two covers.* And remember that the chronological span of the books of the Bible is even longer than that of the examples I have just given.

The temptation is often to reduce that huge variety of texts to one kind of thing: to say it is all *really* law or all *really* history, or all *really* poetry. If it is all really law then the Bible is essentially a book of rules with a little bit of illustrative material around the edges. If the Bible is all history then it is a very interesting record of how Judaism and Christianity got going, with a certain amount about what they thought was necessary in doing that. If it is all poetry then you do not need to take it any more seriously than you take any other kinds of poetry (given that so many people think poetry is just fanciful and decorative, God forgive them). The reality is that as soon as you think you know what the Bible is, you turn the page and it turns into something different.

As soon as you think you know what the Bible is, you turn the page and it turns into something different

How can all of this be addressed by God to us? The simplest way in which we can understand this is the one I have already hinted at: this is what God *wants* you to hear. He wants you to hear law and poetry and history. He wants you to hear the polemic and the visions. He wants you to listen to the letters and to think about the chronicles. And from the earliest days, Christians, like Jews before them and Jews now, wrestle with how exactly you can then say, 'This is the word of the Lord', the communication of God. You cannot just go by surface meanings because surface meanings do not immediately help you with understanding why God wants you to hear it. This may be the word of God, but why exactly is it important to God that you know it?

Let me give you one significant, but partial, analogy from the Bible itself. Jesus in his teaching does not simply pronounce laws. Jesus tells stories. He tells a series of pungent, dramatic little narratives which you have to digest, to allow to work on you; and when that has happened, you have to decide what has changed as a result of hearing the story. Listen to those diverse voices. Observe the interplay of events, and at the end of the parable, where are you now? Because you are not where you were at the beginning. And you have had to look at various characters in the story and try and discover what they tell you about yourself. Quite often with the parables, the question that Jesus leaves us with is, 'Who are you in this story?' Are you the prodigal son who has come home or are you after all the tiresome and self-righteous elder brother standing with arms folded at the door? *Who are you?*

Now, that means that the whole of the story is intended to have an effect. It is intended to draw you in and make you think about yourself in relation to God. It does not mean that Jesus is endorsing everything that everybody in the story says. How could he? When Jesus tells a story about an unjust judge or a murderous tyrant returning to his kingdom and slaughtering his enemies, Jesus is not saying that is a good thing to do. He is telling a story in which such figures appear, and at the end of it he is going to ask you where and who you are.

So, with the parables, it will not help to focus on details in isolation. You need to let the whole thing work upon you. You must not jump to conclusions while the story is still being told. And that, I think, helps just a little bit in thinking about the Bible as a whole. The Bible is, you might say, God telling us a parable or a whole sequence of parables. God is saying, 'This is how people heard me, saw me, responded to me; this is the gift I gave them; this is the response they made … Where are you in this?'

You must not jump to conclusions while the story is still being told

If in that story we find accounts of the responses of Israel to God that are shocking or hard to accept, we do not have to work on the assumption that God *likes* those responses. For example: many of the early Israelites in the Old Testament clearly thought it was God's will that they should engage in 'ethnic cleansing' – that they should slaughter without mercy the inhabitants of the Promised Land into which they had been led. And for centuries, millennia even, people have asked, 'Does that mean that God *orders* or approves of genocide?' If he did, that would be so hideously at odds with what the biblical story as a whole seems to say about God. But if we understand that response as simply part of the story, we see that this is how people thought they were carrying out God's will at the time. The point is to look at God, look at yourself, and to ask where you are in the story. Are you capable – *in the light of the Bible itself as a whole* – of responding more lovingly or faithfully than ancient Israel?

Hearing the whole story

One of the great tragedies and errors of the way people have understood the Bible has been the assumption that what people did in the Old Testament must have been right 'because it's in the Bible'. It has justified violence, enslavement, abuse and suppression of women, murderous prejudice against gay people; it has justified all manner of things we now cannot but as Christians regard as evil. But they are not there in the Bible because God is telling us, 'That's good.' They are there because God is telling us, 'You need to know that that is how some people responded. You need to know that when I speak to human beings things can go very wrong as well as very wonderfully.' God tells us, 'You need to know that when I speak, it isn't always simple to hear, because of what human beings are like.' We need, in other words, to guard against the temptation to take just a bit of the whole story and treat it as somehow a model for our own behaviour. Christians have often been down that road and it has not been a pretty sight. We need rather to approach the Bible as if it were a parable of Jesus. The whole thing is a gift, a challenge and an invitation into a new world, seeing yourself afresh and more truthfully.

Approach the Bible as if it were a parable of Jesus

So God speaks to us by telling us stories. And God does this not just by giving a straight narrative but also by giving examples of how people reacted in their laws, in their proverbs and their songs. We hear his call to us by witnessing its impact on those human beings thousands of years ago. But there is one important difference between the parables and the Bible as a whole. Jesus' parables are simple, contemporary stories. They are drawn from everyday situations. They deal in a very prosaic way for most of the time with the relations of very ordinary people. But the sweep of the Bible's history is much longer. And the Bible is not simply saying, 'Here is a story', but 'Here is *your* story.' Your life began with Noah and Abraham and Moses. Your history goes right back to those beginnings. This is your past we are talking about and the people about whom the Bible stories are written are people who are your family.

A Bible story is, inescapably, about history. It is about how things came into being, and how those things that came into being are still shaping you here and now as a Christian. If you met Abraham you would probably be very surprised. Perhaps one day, in whatever sense God wishes us to do so, we may meet the remote figure who stands behind the sagas about Abraham. But I think it would be a bit of a shock. It would be a little like meeting a long-lost cousin from a very distant country, with a very different culture and language. But it would be even harder than meeting your second cousin from Australia. This is your millionth cousin from prehistoric Mesopotamia. And your first thought would almost certainly be that you have no idea how to relate to him. Yet the Bible says, 'This man is your family and his story is the beginning of your story, and if it were not for him you would not be who you are now. So get used to it …'

This is why history *does* matter in the Bible overall, in a way that doesn't really apply in the parables. When Jesus says that there was once a man who had two sons, then we would regard as a nuisance somebody who put up a hand and asked, 'Where did he live? What was his name?' Such questions a child might ask when told a parable. But with the Bible as a whole it matters that we are not just talking about an abstract case; we are talking about a story that unfolds in particular times and places, leading towards here and now; leading towards us.

Now that brings us to the complicated question of the Bible's historical claims. Is the Bible accurate history? Some people get very anxious indeed about this. Large volumes have been written, trying to show that, for example, what the book of Daniel says about Babylonian history can be squared with what we know about Babylonian history from elsewhere. I admire the ingenuity that goes into this but I am not at all convinced that such people have quite got the right end of the stick. Does God really want us to know, in exact detail, ancient Babylonian history? I suspect not. But I am confident that God does want us to know how people in circumstances of acute displacement, living with the fear and the anxiety of a persecuted minority, responded to a hostile state and a pagan power. And Daniel certainly tells us *that*. He tells us with such force and depth that those stories as much as any in the Old Testament have entered into the imagination of a whole civilization. It is a very few people indeed who do not know something about Daniel in the Lion's Den.

So, what does God want us to know? What does he want to tell us? He wants to tell us that there was a moment in the history of ancient Israel when in the light of the experience of exile and persecution, God's people had to sit down and think and pray and imagine with a new intensity how they could be faithful in such circumstances. God wants us to know that, and he wants us to know what response they came up with, and he wants us to ask ourselves, 'Where are we in this story?' Those stories would not be there had it not been for the reality of Babylon and the reality of exile and the reality of persecution. Yes, history matters, but that does not mean that you should lose your faith because the chronology of King Belshazzar's reign in the book of Daniel does not square with what people dig up in the Middle East on archaeological expeditions.

The chronology of Daniel presents a well-known example of some of the conflicts that can arise, and it illustrates the need to exercise a certain amount of common sense in how we approach the Bible. Rather than get hung up on historical details, we need to keep coming back to the question, 'What does God want to tell us?' If we hang our faith on the absolute historical accuracy of Scripture in every detail, we risk making

Scripture a sort of 'magic' book that turns up the right answers to all sorts of rather irrelevant questions, instead of being a book that gives us, in the wonderful words of the Coronation service, 'the lively oracles of God'. The Bible is not intended to be a mere chronicle of past events, but a living communication from God, telling us *now* what we need to know for our salvation.

The Bible is not intended to be a mere chronicle of past events, but a living communication from God

So, we can see that we need to tread carefully the path between an obsession with historical accuracy, in a way that fails to do justice to the kind of book the Bible is, and a cavalier attitude to history that just says, 'Frankly, it doesn't much matter *what* happened; all that matters is that it's a good story.' Because we are historical beings, because we learn as time passes and we reflect on our past, then it does matter that there was a real historical moment when real people were thinking about Babylon and lions and about the threat of death and the challenge of resistance. It was real then and it is real now.

At the same time, we need to recognize that we are on slightly different ground when it comes to the New Testament. For we are dealing there with texts written very soon after the events they describe. And we are clearly dealing with a complex of tradition that must involve a degree of personal reminiscence. We are not talking about someone in 500 BC telling a story about events that happened in 1500 BC. We are talking instead about an easily measureable lifetime's span. So as a matter of bare fact I would say that the historical ground of the New Testament is of crucial importance. Here we are seeing the impact of God's communication reflected in first- and second-generation reminiscence.

Christ at the centre

And that brings us to Jesus. It is all very well to talk about finding yourself in God's story, about reflecting and imagining; but, as we do all that, how can we decide what a good or bad interpretation of that story might be like? What criteria do we have for discerning truth from falsehood? The Christian answer is, unsurprisingly, in terms of Jesus Christ. As Christians read the Bible, the story converges on Jesus. The full meaning of what has gone before is laid bare in Jesus. The agenda for what follows is set in Jesus. And, without trying to undermine or ignore the integrity of Jewish Scripture in itself (a complex question that needs the most careful and sensitive understanding of the experience and reflection of our Jewish brothers and

As Christians read the Bible, the story converges on Jesus

sisters), the Christian is bound to say that he or she can only read those Jewish Scriptures as moving towards the point at which a new depth of meaning is laid bare in the life, death and resurrection of Jesus.

All these stories, narratives of God's initiative and human response, pivot around that one central fact. Here, in the story of Jesus, is the story in which we see what an unequivocal obedience and love look like. Here is the story where we see a response to God so full of integrity, so whole, that it reflects perfectly the act of God that draws it out. Here is the story in which the speaking of God and the responding of human beings are bound together inseparably. And so if the whole Bible is about the speaking of God and the responding of human beings, then of course it is by looking at the story of Jesus, the luminous centre, that we discover how to read the rest of it. Jesus, living, dying, raised from the dead, breathing his Spirit on his Church – it is in his light that you read the rest of the Bible.

Now, that is a lifetime's work. It is not as if you can produce once and for all a Christ-centred reading of the Bible that tells you exactly how to relate all the different bits to the centre. On the contrary, you keep going round and round, in a kind of virtuous circle. And as you keep circling around that central reality, each time round you may see something fresh. 'Ah, so *that's* how that bit in

Leviticus and that bit in Ezekiel comes alive when you relate it to Jesus.' And the whole massive history of Christian commentary on the Bible is just an ever-expanding exercise in that reality: that of relating different bits to the centre. Those readers who know their business are doing just that: pondering and absorbing the Bible, hoping that something will come alive in relation to Jesus Christ in a new way.

So reading the Bible is about listening to God in Jesus – which is what Christians ought to be doing in all circumstances anyway. It is letting the Holy Spirit bring you inside the story of how God related to the ancient Israelites and the first Christian believers – letting the Holy Spirit bring you inside that story so that you recognize it as *your* story. Suddenly these bizarre and exotic figures from the ancient Near East look you in the eye, and you recognize your own reflection. You see that they are indeed like you and you are like them. Reading the Bible is about building analogies between then and now, and recognizing in them *your* story. And developing and maturing in the reading of the Bible involves coming to recognize patterns of faithful and unfaithful response to God in the light of Jesus. That is what begins to happen when you make Christ the centre and focus of your prayerful reading.

It is important to recognize that this is not some twenty-first-century invention. This process is already going on within the Bible. Let me give you an example from the Old Testament. In the first and second books of Kings we read about the regular struggles that took place between the prophets and the kings of Israel. One of the most dramatic stories there is of the massacre by Jehu of the royal house of Ahab at Jezreel. This story is presented in the second book of Kings as a triumph of God's righteousness. The appalling Jehu, who is a mass murderer on a spectacular scale, obliterates not only the immediate and extended family of King Ahab and Queen Jezebel, but pretty well anyone who has ever exchanged a polite word with them. And he is anointed specifically to do this job by the prophet Elisha.

Now that, clearly, is a rather problematic story because of all the random bloodshed in it. But it did not take twenty Christian centuries for people to notice that. For in the book of the prophet Hosea (1.4) you will find, just a few generations later, a prophet of Israel looking back on that very story and saying that Jezreel is a name of shame in history, not of triumph, and that Jehu's atrocities deserve to be punished. Something has happened to shift the perspective. And I imagine that if asked what he meant, Hosea would have said, 'I'm sure my prophetic forebears were absolutely certain they were doing the will of God. And I'm sure the tyranny and idolatry of the royal house of Ahab was a scandal that needed to be ended. *But*, human beings being what they are, the clear word of God calling Israel to faithfulness and to resistance was so easily turned into an excuse for yet another turn of the screw in human atrocity and violence. And we're right to shed tears for that memory.'

That to me is a very powerful moment in the Old Testament: a recognition that it is possible to grow in understanding and to think again about the past. Something in the world of the prophet Hosea – who writes so movingly about the helpless love of God for God's people, the divine commitment to a love that cannot be given up even when it looks like the sort of love that humiliates the lover – had already opened up the heart to seeing something more of God. And for the Christian, there is in this a sort of foretaste of the terrifying compassion of God that we see in Jesus Christ breaking through.

Reading together

My very last point is one I touched on at the start of this chapter. We read the Bible *together*. The Bible that we read is a Bible that has already been read by countless Christians before us, and is being read by others today.

And so we need to listen not only to what the Bible is saying, but to what it is saying to those around us and those in the past. That is one of the meanings of 'tradition' in the Church. You listen to the way in which people have been reading the Bible. And it is one of the crucially important things about the Church now: that we listen to one another reading the Bible. Now, that can be quite startling. For many people in the 1970s and 1980s it was surprising to realize what the story of the exodus, for example, meant to people in deprived communities in Latin America. And there are many other examples that we could give.

The Bible that we read is a Bible that has already been read by countless Christians before us

So we read together, we hear together. And instead of that picture of the Bible as a book held in the hands of a solitary reader alone in a room, have in your mind another kind of picture, one in which somebody is proclaiming God's story to a gathering of diverse people – and all of them asking themselves, and asking one another, 'How do we find ourselves in this? How are we going to be renewed together by this reading?' Because when that happens, the Bible is an essential *source*, as well as a *sign*, of the Christian life.

For reflection or discussion

1 Choose and read a story from the Bible, and then ask yourself where you are in the story. Why do you see yourself in that way? And how does that affect what you hear God saying through the story?
2 Can you think of an example in the Bible where what we have is a record, not of a word of God to humans but of a human response to God? How would you describe that response? Do you think it is a response that would have pleased God, or not?
3 Why is it important for Christians to read the Bible in the light of the life and teaching of Jesus? Can you think of something that Jesus said or did that makes a difference to how we should interpret another part of the Bible?

3

Eucharist

> Listen! I am standing at the door, knocking: if you hear my voice and open the door, I will come in to you and eat with you, and you with me. (Revelation 3.20)

For Christians, to share in the Eucharist, the Holy Communion, means to live as people who know that they are always *guests* – that they have been welcomed and that they are wanted. It is, perhaps, the most simple thing that we can say about Holy Communion, yet it is still supremely worth saying. In Holy Communion, Jesus Christ tells us that he wants our company.

> *In Holy Communion, Jesus Christ tells us that he wants our company*

The word of welcome

When reading the Gospels you sometimes get the impression that if anywhere in ancient Galilee you heard a loud noise and a lot of laughter and talking and singing, you could be reasonably sure that Jesus of Nazareth was around somewhere nearby. Jesus created fellowship wherever he was. And it is one of the things in the Gospels that is remembered as most distinctive about him, because even then some of his friends were embarrassed by it. The indiscriminate generosity and the willingness to mix with unsuitable people were already, in the first Christian generation, just difficult enough for the Gospel writers to scratch their heads and cough just a little bit about it. But they could not deny it or suppress it. It was too vividly remembered. Jesus sought out company, and the effect of his presence was to create a celebration, to bind people together.

There are many stories about Jesus and hospitality in the Gospels, but there is one in particular that tell us something very crucial about the Eucharist. It is the story in Luke 19 of Jesus' arrival in Jericho and his meeting with Zacchaeus. Zacchaeus the tax collector is worried that he will be unable to see over the heads in the crowd, so he climbs a tree, hoping that nobody will notice. Jesus stops underneath the tree and looks up. You can imagine several thousand pairs of eyes looking up at the same moment towards a scarlet-faced tax collector perched on a branch – and the collective intake of breath when Jesus says to him, 'Aren't you going to ask me to your home?'

In other words Jesus is not only someone who *exercises* hospitality; he *draws out* hospitality from others. By his welcome he makes other people capable of welcoming.

And that wonderful alternation in the Gospels between Jesus giving hospitality and receiving hospitality shows us something absolutely essential about the Eucharist. We are the guests of Jesus. We are there because he asks us, and because he wants our company. At the same time we are set free to invite Jesus into our lives and literally to receive him into our bodies in the Eucharist. His welcome gives us the courage to open up to him. And so the flow of giving and receiving, of welcome and acceptance, moves backwards and forwards without a break. We are welcomed and we welcome; we welcome God and we welcome our unexpected neighbours. That, surely, is one of the wonderful and unique things about the Holy Eucharist. We invoke Jesus and his Spirit, we call him to be present – and we are able to do this only because he has first called us to be present. His way of welcoming Zacchaeus, and his way of welcoming us, is to say, 'Aren't you going to ask me to your home?'

His welcome gives us the courage to open up to him

This giving and receiving of welcome is central to the way in which Jesus' ministry is portrayed in the Gospels. But it is not just an agreeable personal habit that Jesus has, and it is not a decorative addition to the main business of his ministry, a sort of pleasant extra. It is the actual, visible way in which he engages in remaking a community. Who are the real people of God now? The ones who accept Jesus' invitation. Not the ones who fulfil all the cultic demands, not the ones who score highly on the scale of piety, but the ones who are willing to hear him say, 'Aren't you going to ask me home?' It is as simple as that. The meals that Jesus shares in his ministry are the way in which he begins to re-create a community, to lay the foundations for rethinking what the words 'the people of God' mean.

Now, one of the great themes of the resurrection stories in the Gospels is that this starts all over again on the far side of Jesus' death on the cross. One of the essential truths about the resurrection is that Jesus is still doing what he did before; and part of what he is still doing is exactly this offering and accepting of hospitality. When, in Luke's Gospel, Jesus comes through the locked doors to the disciples, the first thing he says after telling them not to be afraid is, 'Aren't you going to give me something to eat?' The disciples, like Zacchaeus, are so stunned by the presence of the Saviour that for a moment they forget the ordinary courtesies and have to be reminded. And just as Zacchaeus scrambles down from the tree and tries to find adequate words for an invitation, so one imagines on Easter Day the disciples hastily and apologetically rummage around in the cupboards until they have found a probably slightly elderly piece of fish.

'Aren't you going to give me something to eat?' It is the same tone of voice as that used with the tax collector, the same miraculous welcome. The resurrected Jesus is doing what he always did. And that is why it is very significant that in the Acts of the Apostles, when the risen Christ is proclaimed, the apostles identify themselves as the witnesses who 'ate and drank with him after he rose from the dead' (Acts 10.41).

We can see, then, that when the risen Christ eats with the disciples it is not just a way of proving he is 'really' there; it is a way of saying that what Jesus did in creating a new community during his earthly life, he is doing now with the apostles in his *risen* life. We who are brought into the company of the apostles in our baptism – which, remember, brings us to where Jesus is to be found – share that 'apostolic' moment when we gather to eat and drink in Jesus' presence. And that is why, throughout the centuries since, Christians have been able to say exactly what the apostles say: they are the people with whom Jesus ate and drank after he was raised from the dead.

Holy Communion makes no sense at all if you do not believe in the resurrection

Holy Communion makes no sense at all if you do not believe in the resurrection. Without the resurrection, the Eucharist becomes simply a memorial meal, recalling a rather sad and overpowering occasion in the upper room. Allegedly, Queen Victoria did not like going to Holy Communion on Easter Sunday, because, she said, she could not understand why you had to interrupt a joyful day with such a sad service. There is indeed a certain sombreness about some ways of celebrating the Eucharist (and a bit later on, I'll suggest why that is not always inappropriate). But the starting point must be where the apostles themselves began, eating and drinking with him after he was raised from the dead, experiencing once again his call into a new level of life together, a new fellowship and solidarity, and a new willingness and capacity to be welcomers themselves.

Celebrating the Eucharist not only reminds us that we are invited to be guests; it also reminds us that we are given the freedom to invite others to be guests as well. We have experienced the hospitality of God in Christ; our lives are therefore set free to be hospitable. You remember that, when we were thinking about baptism, we saw how Christian life brings us into the neighbourhood of human need and human suffering. Thinking now about the Eucharist, we can fill that out a little bit further. Being in the neighbourhood of Jesus is sharing Jesus' freedom to *invite* – to make our lives and our communities places of welcome for those most deeply in need of solidarity, of fellowship. As sharers in the Eucharist, we become involved in Jesus' own continuing work of bridging the gulfs between people, drawing them into shared life, in the light and the strength of his great central task of bridging the gulf between God and humanity created by our selfish, forgetful and fearful habits.

God the Giver

But what about the original event on which the Eucharist is based? The Gospel of Luke tells us that Jesus was sharing a meal for the last time with his friends, and commanded them, 'Do this in remembrance of me' (Luke 22.19). As Jesus meets with his friends for that last supper and tells them to see the broken bread and wine poured out as his body and blood which are about to be broken and poured out in crucifixion, he says in effect, 'What is going to happen to me, the suffering and death I'm about to endure, the tearing of my flesh and the shedding of my blood, is to be the final, the definitive, sign of God's welcome and God's mercy.' Instead of being the ultimate tragedy and disaster, it is an open door into the welcome of the Father. That is what he is saying in the upper room on Maundy Thursday, and that is what he says every time we celebrate the Eucharist in commemoration of his death; in affirmation of his resurrection; in expectation of his coming again. If we look back to the 'Last Supper' as simply a sombre, shadowed occasion, we forget what it is that Jesus actually says and does, pointing us forward into the mystery of both the cross and the resurrection.

A great twentieth-century Roman Catholic writer, the Jesuit Maurice de la Taille, once said that at the Last Supper, Jesus 'makes himself a sign': he declares that the bread and wine, identified with his body and blood, are a sign of the world-changing events of Good Friday and Easter, and so a sign of the future, of God's future and God's promise. By identifying himself with the broken bread and the spilled wine, the broken flesh and the shed blood, Jesus says that this death which is approaching is a door into hope. And it is at that moment, when he is looking forward most clearly and vividly to his death, even before the Garden of Gethsemane casts its shadow, that Jesus *gives thanks*. That is, he connects his experience with the reality of God, because that is what thanksgiving does. When we say thank you to God we connect our own experience with God as Giver. We say that what has happened to us is somehow rooted in the gift of God. And when Jesus gives thanks at that moment before the breaking and spilling, before the wounds and the blood, it is as if he is connecting the darkest places of human experience with God the Giver; as if he is saying that even in these dark places God continues to give, and therefore we must continue to give thanks. And that is why the

Greek word *eucharistia*, ‘thanksgiving’, took root and became the earliest and most widespread name for what Christians do when they meet for Holy Communion: they meet to give thanks, even in the heart of the darkest experience.

So as we give thanks over bread and wine in the presence of the Lord we are – with him and in him – seeking to make that connection between the world and God, between human experience and the divine and eternal Giver. And that means that we begin to look differently at the world around us. If in every corner of experience God the Giver is still at work, then in every object we see and handle, in every situation we encounter, God the Giver is present and our reaction is shaped by this. That is why to take seriously what is going on in the Holy Eucharist is to take seriously the whole material order of the world. It is to see everything in some sense *sacramentally*. If Jesus gives thanks over bread and wine on the eve of his death, if Jesus makes that connection between the furthest place away from God, which is suffering and death, and the giving and outpouring of his Father, and if in his person he fuses those things together, then wherever we are some connection between us and God is possible. All places, all people, all things have about them an unexpected sacramental depth. They open on to God the Giver.

All places, all people, all things have about them an unexpected sacramental depth

And that is why many Christians have found that in reflecting on the Eucharist they begin to see what a Christian attitude to the environment might be. Do we live in the world as if God the Giver were within and behind and in the depths of every moment and every material thing? Well, no, for most of the time we do not. We live on the surface, we see what suits us and serves our goals – as if, instead of having their own depth and integrity, things are there just for us to exploit and abuse. Reverence for the bread and the wine of the Eucharist is the beginning of reverence for the whole world in which the giving of God's glory is pulsating beneath the surface of every moment.

That is also why, although this sometimes has been a controversial element in Christian history, reverence for the bread and the wine has instinctively been felt to be a good thing, something appropriate to Christians. It is why the Book of Common Prayer tells you that you need to consume reverently at the end of Holy Communion what is left over. Here is something of the world that has been identified as carrying the power and love of God to you. Don't just throw it away. Make what you will of this tradition of reverence for the consecrated things; but it does at least suggest that to take seriously the material food of the bread and wine can be the beginning of a proper and grateful reverence before *all* God's material things – a doorway into seeing all things as demanding reverent attention, even contemplation.

Holy Communion changes the way we see things as well as people. It changes how we see the world and, as I have already hinted, it changes how we see one another (as we learn to see our neighbour as God's guest). It reinforces and sustains the hospitality that believers want to show to those in need, and it also obliges us to look at other Christians and take seriously the fact that they have been invited too. One of the most transformingly surprising things about Holy Communion is that it obliges you to see the person next to you as *wanted by God*. God wants that person's company as well as mine. How much simpler if God only wanted *my* company and that of those *I* had decided to invite. But God does not play that particular game. And the transforming effect of looking at other Christians as people whose company God wants, is – by the look of things – still sinking in for a lot of Christians, and taking rather a long time …

It does not solve all our problems and disputes. It does not give us a master plan for Christian unity. But it surely helps us to see that there is a difference between looking at another Christian and saying, 'There is somebody *trying to persuade* God to love them (and not succeeding)', and 'There is someone whose *company is desired* by God.' Holy Communion changes the way we see things. One of the gifts we receive at Holy Communion is that gift of new vision: the gift of seeing things – we have to dare to say it just for a moment – from God's perspective.

Honest repentance

I mentioned earlier that there was an element of the sombre in Holy Communion that we cannot entirely avoid: because one of the things that we see at the Lord's Table is ourselves. We are taken back to a last supper at which Jesus identified his betrayer. And in some of the orders of Holy Communion, like the Book of Common Prayer, the narrative is introduced with the words '... in the night in which he was *betrayed*...' We are there as God's guests, there because God loves to have us there, because Jesus has requested the pleasure of our company. But we are also there as those who have the capacity to betray. 'The hand of the one who betrays me is on the table with me,' says Jesus. And he dips the bread in the sauce and passes it to Judas. He warns all those around the table that in a couple of hours' time they are going to abandon him.

That too is part of what is going on at the Eucharist. The Eucharist reminds us of the need for honest repentance – of the need to confront our capacity to betray and forget the gift we have been given. And that is why the Eucharist is not, in Christian practice, a reward for good behaviour; it is the food we need to prevent ourselves from starving as a result of our own self-enclosure and self-absorption, our pride and our forgetfulness.

In many of our churches it was once thought that receiving Holy Communion was something you should only do when you felt you had made 'proper' preparation. There was a time in the nineteenth-century Roman Catholic Church when weekly communion was something your confessor might allow you to undertake if he thought you were doing well. And there is still, in many parts of the Christian world, a kind of assumption that Holy Communion is something for 'the holy'. All that I have said so far should remind us that Holy Communion is no kind of reward: it is, like everything about Jesus Christ, a free gift. We take Holy Communion not because we are doing well, but because we are doing badly. Not because we have arrived, but because we are travelling. Not because we are right, but because we are confused and wrong. Not

We take Holy Communion not because we are doing well, but because we are doing badly

because we are divine, but because we are human. Not because we are full, but because we are hungry.

And so that element of self-awareness and repentance is completely bound up with the nature of what we are doing in the Holy Eucharist: the celebration and the sorrow, the Easter and the cross are always there together. And as we come together as Christians, we come not to celebrate ourselves and how well we are doing, but to celebrate the eternal Gift that is always there, and to give the thanks that are drawn out of us by that Gift.

Holy Communion, then, is the way in which the whole of the Gospel story is played out in our midst. You remember that, in thinking about the Bible, we recognized those biblical figures in the remote past as part of our own family. In Holy Communion that becomes something very immediate, something enacted very physically: we are members of the same kindred and, here and now, guests at the same table. We are experiencing Jesus creating community by his welcome, but we are also, with the patriarchs and apostles, those who are liable to forget, betray and run. We are the ones who are called back and invited afresh on the resurrection day to experience yet again the creation of community, even through death and even through betrayal, abandonment and denial. And we are now the ones who, as we receive Holy Communion, are commissioned to renew the face of the earth. We are those who can see humanity and the whole material world in a fresh way, seeing people and things sacramentally, seeing the depth within them, where the giving of God is always at work.

The transforming Spirit

And so our perspectives open out still further. Holy Communion is not only about our redemption, it is about our creation. It is about an immense and glorious debt that we can never repay: the debt to our creator for our very being. God has called us into being because he wants our company, and redemption would make no sense if it were not the same creative longing for our company that was involved, the creating and transforming Spirit of God calling us once again into life because of that eternal 'desire' for our company – not a divine need that we are summoned into existence to satisfy, but an overflowing divine generosity that seeks to share itself more and more with what is other.

In everything we say about Holy Communion we are talking about the work of the Holy Spirit

In everything we say about Holy Communion we are talking about the work of the Holy Spirit. In the Gospels the Holy Spirit is the living breath of the God who brings Jesus alive – literally, at the beginning of his life in Mary's womb, fully alive to his vocation at his baptism, alive out of death after the descent to the realm 'where all things are forgotten', in the words of the psalm. And that Spirit-given life he then communicates to his people.

So it is that in Holy Communion we invoke and celebrate the action of the Spirit. At the central moment, just before we receive the bread and wine, we pray the prayer of Jesus: we say, 'Our Father . . .' – and that is a great and significant moment, not just a bit of muttered devotion before we start on our way to the altar, but one of the supreme transitions in the drama of the entire service. For when we pray the prayer of Jesus, the Holy Spirit is in us and at work in us. We are affirming that in this act of worship the Holy Spirit is speaking Jesus' words in us, praying 'Abba, Father', as Jesus did and does.

At the same time we recognize and affirm that the transformation that is going on in Holy Communion is the work of the Holy Spirit. We call down the Holy Spirit upon ourselves and upon the gifts of bread and wine: we say, 'Here we are, in the company of Jesus: Father, send the Holy Spirit that as these people share these things, the life of Jesus may fill them all.'

It is not just that we ask the Holy Spirit to effect a miraculous change in the bread and wine. We ask the Holy Spirit to effect a miraculous change in all of *us*, to make us capable of receiving these gifts, and as we receive them to go out, 'in the power of the Spirit to live to God's praise and glory'. So the Holy Spirit, who always brings Jesus alive in our midst, is very specially at work in the Eucharist, making it a means of spiritual transformation. Because of this we go from the table to the work of transfiguring the world in God's power: to seeing the world in a new light, to seeing human beings with new eyes, and to working as best we can to bring God's purpose nearer to fruition in the world.

The Church has not always seen the Eucharist in this globally transforming way. But again and again, the great thinkers and poets have seen into that depth and said yes, the Eucharist is somehow a revelation of God's final act and purpose. It is, we might say, the beginning of the end of the world. That is quite a lot to carry with us to the Lord's table. But this is where we see the Holy Spirit working, to bring the end of the world closer. Yet that dimension of hope for the end, that dimension of an anticipation of what God will do with all people and all things, that sense that the transformation going on in the Eucharist is just a glimpse of the transformation of all things – all of this is surely one of the things that makes the Eucharist so vital and central in our Christian devotion. It is what makes it so much the appropriate sign of the baptized life, because it is the material sign of a new creation, a new phase in the world's history that is moving towards God's final purpose with new energy and focus. And it is also what makes it so much the appropriate context for the hearing and reading of the Bible. It is, as some modern Christian thinkers have said, what makes the Church what it really is. For that short time, when we gather as God's guests at God's table, the Church becomes what it is meant to be – a community of strangers who have become guests together and are listening together to the invitation of God.

When we gather as God's guests at God's table, the Church becomes what it is meant to be

Sometimes, after receiving Holy Communion, as I look around a congregation, large or small, I have a sensation I can only sum up as *this is it* – this is the moment when people see one another and the world properly: when they are filled with the Holy Spirit and when they are equipped to go and do God's work. It may last only a few seconds, but there it is. It has happened and it happens again and again. And what is the appropriate response? I have already said: *thanksgiving*. Because one of the ways in which the Eucharist overflows into the rest of our life is precisely in giving us that energy and vision for thanksgiving in all things, for making the connection between God the Giver and everything we experience.

This emphatically doesn't mean that we look at everything and just say, 'Oh, that is just how God wants it to be', and pass on, expecting nothing to change. It certainly does not mean we look at situations of suffering and terror and say, 'That is what God wants.' It is about having the capacity to see into the depth of a situation or person and recognize that somewhere in there is God the Giver; and so there is the possibility of more and more giving on the part of God which will bring something new and transforming. And somehow, as I struggle to change myself, the person I am with, the situation I am experiencing, I find that what I am looking for, what I am opening myself to, is that buried reality: God the Giver, who is never exhausted.

In the Eucharist we are at the *centre* of the world: we are where Christ, the Son, gives his life to his Father in the Spirit. And in the Eucharist we are at the *end* of the world: we are seeing how the world's calling is fulfilled in advance; we are seeing ourselves and our world as they really are, contemplating them in the depths of God, finding their meaning in relation to God. And the job of a Christian is constantly trying to dig down to that level of reality, and to allow gratitude, repentance and transformation to well up from that point. 'With you is the fountain of life', says the psalm; and it is that fountain that we drink from in Holy Communion.

For reflection or discussion

1. How do you become more aware of yourself as a guest at the Lord's table? What do you have in common with the other guests?
2. In what sense is the Eucharist a service of thanksgiving, and why?
3. Why does receiving Holy Communion help you to see the world differently? What difference does that make to the way you live as a Christian?

Beacon Books/Kingdom Krafts
30 Madoc Street
Llandudno
LL30 2TL
Tel: 01492 877995
www.beaconbooksandkrafts.co.uk

Date 16/07/14

------------CUSTOMER INVOICE------------
JEL001 = REV JELL

Paid In Full

BEING CHRISTIAN
1 @ 7.99 7.99

NETT	:	7.99
VAT	:	0.00
TOTAL	:	7.99
CASH	:	10.00
CHANGE	:	2.01

Total number of items sold = 1

Staff Name MARIAN Time 14:57
Receipt No. 129372 Till No. 2

Thank you
10% Loyalty Card Available Ask For Details
Kingdom Krafts Charity No: 1051917

4

Prayer

> He was praying in a certain place, and after he had finished, one of his disciples said to him, 'Lord, teach us to pray ...' He said to them, 'When you pray, say:
> Father, hallowed be your name.
> Your kingdom come.
> Give us each day our daily bread.
> And forgive us our sins,
> for we ourselves forgive everyone indebted to us.
> And do not bring us to the time of trial.' (Luke 11.1–4)

The fourth and last of our 'Christian essentials' is prayer, and in particular the need for us all to *grow* in prayer. Growing in prayer is not simply acquiring a set of special spiritual skills that operate in one bit of your life. It is about growing into what St Paul calls 'the measure of the full stature of Christ' (Ephesians 4.13). It is growing into the kind of humanity that Christ shows us. Growing in prayer, in other words, is growing in Christian humanity.

> *Growing in prayer is growing in Christian humanity*

It seems that all Christian reflection, all theology worth the name, began as people realized that because of Jesus

Christ they could talk to God in a different way. It was the new experience of Christian prayer that got people thinking, 'If Jesus somehow makes it possible for us to talk to God in a new way, then surely there are things we ought to be saying and believing about Jesus.' And so the great exploratory business of theology began to unfold.

That newness of prayer is expressed most vividly by St Paul in Romans 8 and Galatians 4. 'God has sent the Spirit of his Son into our hearts, crying, "Abba! Father!"' (Galatians 4.6). The new way we talk to God is as Father, and that is the work of the Spirit of Jesus. And of course it is the prayer recorded of Jesus himself, the night before his death (Mark 14.36). So, for the Christian, to pray – before all else – is *to let Jesus' prayer happen in you*. And the prayer that Jesus himself taught his disciples expresses this very clearly: 'Our Father'. We begin by expressing the confidence that we stand where Jesus stands and we can say what Jesus says.

Some kinds of instruction in prayer used to say, at the beginning, 'Put yourself in the presence of God.' But I often wonder whether it would be more helpful to say, 'Put yourself in the place of Jesus.' It sounds appallingly ambitious, even presumptuous, but that is actually what the New Testament suggests we do. Jesus speaks to God *for* us, but we speak to God *in him*. You may say what you want – but *he* is speaking to the Father, gazing into the depths of the Father's love. And as you understand Jesus better, as you grow up a little in your faith, then what you want to say gradually shifts a bit more into alignment with what he is always saying to the Father, in his eternal love for the eternal love out of which his own life streams forth.

That, in a nutshell, is prayer – letting Jesus pray in you, and beginning that lengthy and often very tough process by which our selfish thoughts and ideals and hopes are gradually aligned with his eternal action; just as, in his own earthly life, *his* human fears and hopes and desires and emotions are put into the context of his love for the Father, woven into his eternal relation with the Father – even in that moment of supreme pain and mental agony that he endures the night before his death.

So it should not surprise us that Jesus begins his instructions on prayer by telling us to affirm that we stand where he stands: 'Our Father'. Everything that follows is bathed in the light of that relationship. The Lord's Prayer begins with a vision of a world that is transparent to God: 'May your kingdom come, your will be done; may what you (God) want shine through in this world and shape the kind of world it is going to be.' And only when we

Jesus begins his instructions on prayer by telling us to affirm that we stand where he stands

have begun with that affirmation, that imagining of a world in which God's light is coming through, only then do we start asking for what we need. And what do we need? We need sustenance, mercy, protection, daily bread, forgiveness; we need to be steered away from the tests that we are not strong enough to bear.

A great deal of the very earliest Christian reflection on prayer after the New Testament period is based firmly on the Lord's Prayer. 'Teach us to pray,' say the disciples to Jesus, and Jesus gives them the Lord's Prayer; so it is obviously a good place to begin. In the rest of this chapter, I want to try and offer a brief overview of three early Christian writers who speak and write about prayer starting from this point. One of them is a theological scholar and teacher, one of them is a bishop, and one of them is a monk, and they belong, roughly, to the third, fourth and fifth centuries of the Christian era.

'The whole of our life says, **Our Father'** *(Origen)*

My first example, the theological teacher, is Origen, who died probably in 254. He grew up in Alexandria in Egypt, and taught in various places around the eastern Mediterranean, especially in Alexandria and Caesarea in Palestine. For a lot of his career he was a layman, but he was eventually ordained in Palestine (rather to the alarm of some people who thought he was very unsound); he was imprisoned in the great persecutions of the 250s, and seems to have died as a result of the torture and injuries he endured in prison. Not just an academic, then, but a witness who carried the cross in his own life and death.

Origen's little book on prayer is the first really systematic treatment of the subject by a Christian. And one of the questions he asks is one you have probably asked yourself from time to time: 'If God knows what we are going to ask, why bother to pray?' (You may be relieved to know that they were already asking that in the third century.) And Origen has as good an answer as anyone has given: God knows, of course, what we are going to say and do, but God has decided that he will work out his purposes *through* what we decide to say and do. So, if it is God's will to bring something about, some act of healing or reconciliation, some change for the better in the world, he has chosen that your prayer is going to be part of a set of causes that makes it happen. So you'd better get on with it, as you and your prayer are part of God's overall purpose for the situation in which he is going to work.

It is a pretty good answer – and it is one that certainly keeps us on our knees working hard: which is just as well. But Origen also gives us lots of practical advice about how to do it. He tells us, for example, that we should start our prayer with praise: tell God why he matters: because you need to know that, even if God doesn't. End with thanks. And on the basis of the psalms – 'In the evening, and morning, and at noonday will I pray' (Psalm 55.18, BCP) – pray at least three times a day.

These are very straightforward bits of advice. But when we then turn to what Origen says specifically about the Lord's Prayer, we discover a great treasury of profound insight. In a very New Testament way, he stresses the spirit of adoption we have received: we speak to God as daughters and sons, and so we speak to God as a God who has – through his own freedom – decided not to be remote, but immediate. He has decided to be our *friend* – indeed, the word in Greek can be even stronger, our lover – the one who really embraces us and is as close as we can imagine. Very near the heart of Christian prayer is getting over the idea that God is somewhere a very, very long way off, so that we have to shout very loudly to be heard. On the contrary: God has decided to be an intimate friend and he has decided to make us part of his family, and we always pray on that basis.

The heart of Christian prayer is getting over the idea that God is somewhere a very, very long way off

With that in mind, Origen reminds us that our prayer is always *in* Jesus rather than *to* Jesus. Then, as now, plenty of people were in the habit of chatting to Jesus as a friend – which is fine in its way; but the essence of prayer as the New Testament presents it is to let Jesus pray in you and take you into the very heart of God the Father. Just as Jesus empties himself out of love for us, we, in return, empty ourselves. We push away the selfish desires and the limiting images that crowd into our heads. We make room, we empty our minds and hearts, so that the love of God can fill them. So our prayer is that we may be made one with the will and the action of Jesus. And that means, says Origen, that when we pray we are all of us 'priests'. Just as Jesus bears up the suffering and grief of the world to God, so when we pray and join in his activity we are doing a priestly thing, bringing the pains and needs of earth into the heart of God. And as we pray, therefore, we become images of Jesus the priest. Remember what we were thinking about in relation to becoming 'priestly' through our baptism: the same point is being made here.

Origen has more practical advice: you can pray anywhere, he says, don't imagine it's restricted to special places. But that does not mean that prayer is just a casual matter; physical stillness and physical solitude *matter*. Interestingly, he says that it is not just about you as a individual being still and quiet in preparation for prayer; you need to be quiet at a deeper level – that is to say, you need to be at peace with other people before you embark on prayer. So, he tells us, do your fasting, do your giving – and do your reconciliation: because that is as essential a part of prayer as being quiet. If you are tempted to think that Origen is drifting off into mystical abstraction, remember that *being ready to pray is being at peace with other people*. Be reconciled and then come and offer your gift, as Jesus says (Matthew 5.24). And in one of his sermons on Leviticus, Origen underlines the fact that generosity to the needy is part of the purification that prayer requires.

Behind all this there is quite a complicated scheme in Origen's mind, spelled out in many of his longer works, which is all about detaching your spirit – the essential you – from the passions and instincts and desires that crowd in on you. You need to step back from the kind of *reactive* life that just lets your emotions and instincts splurge out in all directions. Be aware; be on guard that your spirit may not be smothered by a welter of thoughts and emotions.

In another sermon – this time on the book of Numbers – Origen talks about the journey of the Israelites out of slavery in Egypt as a symbol for our journey to God. Egypt is a place of temptation; Egypt, as the Bible reminds us, is a place where you find fleshpots. But as soon as you have left the fleshpots of Egypt behind, it is not all plain sailing.

You go into the desert and into a period of struggle. You go into uncharted territory and an uncertain future, and you have got to learn discernment, how to tell good from bad. You have got to learn vision and knowledge. All being well, that inner freedom will lead to what he calls 'sober drunkenness', where you are 'out of your mind' – removed from your ordinary selfish, anxious, defensive habits. Your ordinary orientations and instincts have fallen away – and you don't quite know whether you are going to stay upright when you next put your foot on the ground. You do not quite know where you are going, but there is something so exciting and intoxicating about it that you know you are in a different world. It is a long job and the travel through the desert takes many years; but at the end of the journey is freedom.

Out of all this there begins to emerge a model that becomes very popular in the early Church, a threefold pattern of learning to pray. You start with the 'practical' life: learning ordinary self-awareness, the common sense of the Christian life; recognizing when you are being selfish and stupid, and acting instead with an increasing degree of generosity. You move on from that to the freedom to see God in the world around you. When you have got your ego and all its fussiness a little bit in its place, then actually you see more; the world is more real and more beautiful. You see order and pattern in it, and your heart and your imagination expand until at last you arrive in the third level, at what Origen rather unpromisingly calls 'theology' (by which he does not mean a degree in religious studies!). The intensity and clarity of what you see in the world around you triggers a sort of 'leap in the dark' – or rather into the light – and into God. Your vision is clarified; your actions are gradually disciplined; the divine life slowly transforms you; and, to use one of the best expressions that Origen comes up with, we move into a condition where 'The whole of our life says, *Our Father*'.

Your vision is clarified; your actions are gradually disciplined; the divine life slowly transforms you

'Prayer heals relations' (Gregory of Nyssa)

Just over a hundred years later than Origen we find another Greek-speaking writer building on some of what Origen says, but turning it in a few new directions as well. This time it is a bishop from Asia Minor called Gregory of Nyssa. He was a very important philosopher and theologian in his day, and one of his best and most enduring works is a commentary on the Lord's Prayer.

One of the very first things Gregory says in this book is very close to one of Origen's themes: prayer is in significant part about resolving conflict and rivalry. If people prayed seriously they would be reconciled. It is a very simple thing, but it is worth thinking about. Prayer, for Gregory, takes us into heaven, it gives us direct access in Christ to the Father and makes us equal to the angels (or even better) because God's glory is open to us. And when we pray we gradually receive a share in God's power. Now that sounds very exciting, because if we have a share in God's power then we can go and do miracles. Well, yes indeed (says Gregory): you *can* go and do miracles – like forgiving your neighbours, and giving your property away to the poor, because *that* is how God exercises power. And if we are having a share in God's power, that is where our prayer will lead.

Gregory was probably the first writer to make the point that the most daunting part of the Lord's Prayer is the section, 'Forgive us our sins, as we forgive those who sin against us' – or rather, literally, 'As we *have* forgiven those who sin against us'. It is certainly pretty presumptuous to say to God, 'Forgive me my sins. Look, I have forgiven the people who sinned against me!' The parable of the debtors in the New Testament suggests that God responds with the divine equivalent of a rather quizzical look. But Gregory makes of it a very bold and slightly mischievous image: he says, in effect, 'When you're teaching children things, you first say, "Watch me do this"; but later you'll be saying, "Now *you* do it, now *you* show me."' And God is doing that to us. He has offered his forgiveness and then he steps back and says, 'Now then, *you* show me.' Gregory says that it is not simply that we are called to be imitators of God: God is asked to be an imitator of us: 'Forgive me. I have forgiven.' Gregory leaves us in no doubt that *that* is one of the most difficult bits of the prayer and yet one of the most important. Because it shows so clearly what we are supposed to be doing with the freedom God wants to give us.

As you might expect from what I have already said, Gregory insists that we should not get too introspective about some of the other bits of the prayer. Consider the line, 'Give us this day our daily bread.' Well (says Gregory), is that about *my* getting what *I* need? Actually, no. Because the bread of God that comes down from heaven and gives life to the world (in the words of St John's Gospel) is *everybody's* bread. I am asking for bread for everyone. And I can only say that I have properly received my daily bread (he says) 'if no one goes hungry or distressed because you are satisfied'. I receive my daily bread when no one is made poor because I am rich. So the resolve to work for justice along with reconciliation is essentially part of living out the Lord's Prayer.

You could sum up what Gregory says about the Lord's Prayer simply by saying, 'Prayer heals relations.' Prayer is about reconciliation, justice, and how it changes your attitude to other people and the world. Prayer is not a narrowly private activity; it is about your *belonging* in the body of Christ, and in the family of humanity. If you understand what is going on when you pray, then the world changes. And if in prayer you are gradually becoming attuned to the will and purpose of God, then the divine power that comes into you is bound to find its outlet in this healing of relations. That is not to say that you pray *in order to be* a nicer person, or so that justice and reconciliation will happen. You pray *because Christ is in you*. And if that is really happening, then the sort of things you can expect to see developing around you are justice and reconciliation.

Now, for Gregory, as for Origen, one of the most crucial aspects of prayer is to understand it as a constant growth, a constant movement into an endless mystery. He says in his book on the life of Moses that the only definition of life with God is that it has *no* definition in the sense of having a boundary around it. You keep on moving. There is always more to discover. And so just as Moses goes up into the darkness on top of Mount Sinai to meet God, so our journey out of Egypt, through the desert, up the mountain, is a journey into darkness where our ideas about God tend to fall away. And yet it is in the depths of darkness – recognizing we shall never master

In the depths of darkness – recognizing we shall never . . . understand what God is like – enlightenment comes

or understand what God is like – that enlightenment comes.

It is a little bit like the experience that the Zen Buddhists speak of when they have sat with the paradox or the riddle for such a long time that they finally realize that they are never going to solve it; *then* enlightenment happens. So with Gregory, when you have sat in the darkness and recognized, 'I shall never get on top of this', then you might suddenly realize in the depth of your being that you *see* what you thought you were not meant to see. It is 'ecstasy', though not quite what we might mean by the word. 'Ecstasy' literally means 'standing outside', and here it means standing outside the conventional ways in which we tend to think about ourselves and God.

'O God, make speed to save me' (John Cassian)

My third example is someone in the same tradition as the two we have already considered, but this time someone who bridges a great many different worlds. He is the monk named John Cassian. He had come probably from southern Russia to Egypt to be a monk, and he did most of his writing at the beginning of the fifth century. In

Egypt he had met some of the most famous monastic teachers of his era, and had gone from there across the Mediterranean to found a monastery at Marseilles. The extent of his travel experience meant that he could distil some of the wisdom of the Christian East and bring it into the West. From Marseilles came the monasteries that were founded in southern France. From Marseilles and other Mediterranean ports monks travelled on little expeditions to outlandish places such as Ireland and Cornwall and Wales, and started monasteries there.

Cassian provides for Western Christians a sort of convenient, organized summary of the teaching of the great monks of Egypt. He does this by presenting his teaching in the form of a number of 'conversations'. Instead of just doing straight exposition, Cassian does it in a more 'dramatic' mode. He introduces you to a little group of monks in the desert, talking about a particular theme. Hence the title of his *Book of Conversations* or 'conferences'. It is a sequence of conversations among experienced people about prayer, and they still make very good reading. And it is in the ninth and the tenth books of the *Conversations* that we read his reflections on the Lord's Prayer.

Cassian begins by saying that prayer takes for granted that you have been working on your self-awareness, your emotions, and all the rest of it. Prayer takes for granted

> *Prayer takes for granted that you have been working on your self-awareness*

the 'practical' life, in the sense already sketched, where you have been monitoring your reactions and trying to educate your emotions, and also practising justice and generosity. And it takes for granted that you have a certain level of freedom from the memory of various preoccupations of daily life, and that you are not going to be consumed by anxiety when you get down to prayer. Clear your mind, he says; and then there is a fourfold process to go through. He picks up four words that St Paul uses for prayer, and gives each of them a slightly different meaning. When you have done all that preparatory work, start with *supplication*, open up your need to God. And then make an act of *commitment*. Prayer, he says, is a promise, a pledge: when I pray, I say to God, 'You're there for me: I'm going to be here for you.' And when you have settled into that commitment, that resolution to be there and stay there, that leads on to *intercession* as a mark of the love that rises out of that commitment, and then on to *thanksgiving*, which is not just thanking God for the good things he has done for you, but absorbing his goodness.

We can see some parallels with what Origen says: you move towards thanksgiving, and you understand thanksgiving as something more than just private acknowledgement of God's goodness; you have to learn to approach it as a 'soaking-in' of what God *is*. 'We give thanks to thee for thy great glory', as the Prayer Book has it. When all these things come together (says Cassian) we are on fire with the Holy Spirit. And when we look at Jesus we see someone whose entire life is on fire in that way, with the Spirit.

So when Cassian reflects on the Lord's Prayer, he begins by recognizing that we are adopted children, and as such we have a passionate attachment to our home. We want to be where Christ is fully present: this is our home in the deepest sense. We are alive with longing for heaven. Like Gregory of Nyssa he also notes the seriousness of inviting God to forgive us as we have forgiven. And he has a go at solving another of the great problems that people have: what does it mean to pray, 'Lead us not into temptation'? Surely God does not *make* us be tempted? Cassian says that in the Bible, holy people are tempted all the time, but being *led* into temptation would be like being dropped into it, with no way out. This is what we pray to be defended from. God never drops us into the heart of temptation with no equipment to face it and no way out. And here Christ is always our model, as he prays that God's will should be done in the middle of the most indescribable pressure and pain. He is exposed to temptation but not led into it unprepared; we pray that his life in us may be strong enough to help us survive.

As we move through this process of praying we are likely to find ourselves overtaken with quite a bit of emotional churning. We will be shaken by it. We may find ourselves in tears both of repentance and of joy, because something is going on in us, the landscape is being changed. Prayer, more and more, is not something *we* do, but what we are *letting God* do in us. And when that happens, it is not surprising that we get a bit wobbly and our emotions become a bit tempestuous, and we become baffled and depressed as well. So don't panic! For when those disturbances are going on, it is very likely that God is beginning to settle down more deeply in you.

Prayer, more and more, is not something *we* do, but what we are *letting God* do in us

'Let your prayer,' says Cassian, 'be frequent and brief.' If you try too soon to spend three hours in intense contemplation, the chances are you'll end up with cramp and lots of distractions. You'll find other things to think of apart from God. But by 'frequent and brief' he does not mean just uttering the odd casual word. 'Frequent' is serious, and means 'Keep at it: make it habitual.' But also: don't try and pile up the 'prayer hours' for the sake of thinking that you are doing well. Instead, remember that what you are moving towards is finally the relationship of Jesus to the Father. 'That union of the Father and Son and the Son with the Father will fill our senses and our minds,' he writes. Notice the phrasing: it is once again about being an embodied person living in a particular place and yet seeing all that is around you in the light of God, because prayer has become habitual.

There is one more significant thing to mention about Cassian, and that is his advice about how to become settled in prayer and keep our minds anchored when they are inclined to fly off in different directions. We need a formula. We need a simple, very brief form of words that just calls us back to where we belong. This is the beginning of that long tradition – especially in the Eastern Christian world – that we associate with the so-called 'Prayer of Jesus', the repeated prayer, 'Lord Jesus Christ, Son of God, have mercy on me, a sinner.' But Cassian suggests an even shorter formula: 'O God, make speed to save me' – the words that, in a very slightly different form, begin Morning and Evening Prayer in the Prayer Book, and that echo the words of Psalm 40.13: 'O LORD, make haste to help me.' That is all you need to say, says Cassian; then he adds, in effect, 'and believe me, you will need to say it.' So when you find your mind drifting off, when in a period that you have tried to devote to prayer you find yourself thinking, 'I must check my emails' or 'Did I leave the gas on?' just say, 'O God, make speed to save me', and keep at it. To be faithful to that one phrase is a sign of the fact that you are serious and committed and you have promised to be there.

In the end, prayer

Origen, Gregory and Cassian: those three great figures of the early Church each reflect in different ways on the Lord's Prayer, and each brings into focus three things that are essential to what most Christians have thought about prayer. First, and most importantly, prayer is God's work in us. It is not us trying to persuade God to be nice to us or to get God interested in us. It is opening our minds and hearts and saying to the Father, 'Here is your Son, praying in me through the Holy Spirit. Please listen to him, because I want him to be working, acting and loving in me'.

Second, there is the deep connection that all these writers see between praying and living justly in the world: being the kind of mature human being who is not trapped by selfishness, fear of others, anxiety about the future or the desire to succeed at others' expense. Prayer is the life of Jesus coming alive in you, so it is hardly surprising if it is absolutely bound

Prayer is the life of Jesus coming alive in you

up with a certain way of being human which is about reconciliation, mercy, and freely extending the welcome and the love of God to others.

Third, prayer from our point of view is about fidelity, faithfulness, sticking to it. I may not quite know what is going on; as prayer deepens in me I am less and less likely to know what is going on. I may be baffled, I may be depressed, and I may feel that absolutely nothing is happening: fine. Just stay there and if in doubt say, 'O God, make speed to save me.' Prayer is your promise and pledge to be there for the God who is there for you. And that, essentially, is where prayer for the Christian begins and ends.

For reflection or discussion

1. Growing in prayer is about becoming more and more attuned to God's will – until, like Jesus, you can say, 'The whole of my life says, "Our Father".' Which parts of your life do you feel you need to work on to make that more of a reality?
2. Think of the important relationships in your life. Think also of the relations between people and groups that you know in the wider world. Are any in need of healing? If so, how might your prayer help in that process?

3 Take a few minutes to become settled, still and silent. Detach yourself from the thoughts and feelings that crowd in on you. Slow down your breathing and, as you gently breathe in and out, repeat to yourself, [in] 'O God, [out] make speed to save me.' Or breathe in silently and say to yourself as you breathe out, 'Lord Jesus Christ, Son of God, have mercy on me, a sinner.' Do that for as long as you need to slow the rhythms of your breathing and heartbeat, and then continue with the rest of your prayer.

Suggestions for further reading

These have some demanding bits in them, but are mostly accessible to the general reader.

Scott Hahn, *Letter and Spirit: From Written Text to Living Word in the Liturgy*, New York, Doubleday, 2005.

Timothy Radcliffe, *Why Go to Church? The Drama of the Eucharist,* London, Continuum, 2008.

Alexander Schmemann, *For the Life of the World: Sacraments and Orthodoxy*, Crestwood, New York, St Vladimir's Seminary Press, 1974.

Alexander Schmemann, *Of Water and the Spirit: A Liturgical Study of Baptism*, Crestwood, New York, St Vladimir's Seminary Press, 1974.

Kenneth Stevenson, *Take, Eat: Reflections on the Eucharist*, Norwich, Canterbury Press, 2008.

Translations of early Christian works

St John Cassian, *Conferences* (esp. 9 and 10), translated by Colm Luibheid, New York/Mahwah, Paulist Press, 1985.

St Gregory of Nyssa, *The Lord's Prayer and the Beatitudes*, translated by Hilda Graef, no. 18 in the Ancient

Christian Writers series, London, Longman 1954, various reprints).

Origen, 'On prayer', in J. E. Oulton and Henry Chadwick (eds), *Alexandrian Christianity*, no. 2 in the Library of Christian Classics, London, SCM Press, 1954, various reprints. There is also a (rather less good) translation by William A. Curtis available online.